The Little Sky Angel

For parents, children, and family members that have experienced a loss of a baby.

Written by: Chenna

Copyright © 2022 by Chenna
Illustration: Danushka Sampath

Publisher's Note

Printed and bound in the United States of America. All rights reserved. Published by Guided Corner Stories. No part of this book may be reproduced or transmitted in any form or by any means, electronic or mechanical, including photocopying, recording, or by any information storage and retrieval system except by a review who may quote brief passages in a review to be printed in a magazine, newspaper, or on the Web without permission in writing from the publisher.

Although the author and publisher have made every effort to ensure the accuracy and completeness of information contained in this book, we assume no responsibility for errors, inaccuracies, omissions, or any inconsistency herein. Neither the publisher nor the author shall be liable for damages arising from here.

Dedicated to baby *Akindejoye*
(A-keen-dey-joy-yay)

...and every rainbow baby in Heaven.

There once was an angel that lived in the sky.
And every so often she would spread her wings and fly.

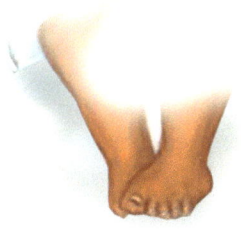

Up, up, up, and above the clouds.
The little sky angel flew without a sound.

She loved the smell of the morning dew that dripped onto the earth.

She bounced all around and basked in the warmth of the sun.

Every so often, she would take a dive down. "**Whoosh,**" and in one flap, she would soar to the ground.

There in the kitchen was a woman singing from below.

Perked with curiosity, she flew closer to the woman's door.

The sound got louder and louder and tickled her ears. She inched towards the woman as she could not help but to listen in.

Suddenly... these musical notes wrapped the little sky angel up.

It bundled and swaddled her until she was nice and tucked.

The little sky angel and the woman then decided to make a song.

"Lub dub ...lub dub," was the beat that went on.

Together they shared so many lovable moments. They danced, laughed, and even got into a little bit of trouble.

Whenever the woman smiled the little sky angel kicked with joy.

It made her so happy to live in a new home.

Every day that passed, the little sky angel grew and grew. There were so many new noises, sounds, and moods.

The woman began planning for others to hear their song. It was almost time to showcase their grand performance.

The little sky angel tried and tried but grew tired too soon.

No sound could be heard. They just could not find the right tune.

Then the little sky angel realized that she could no longer stay below.

The clouds missed her bouncing, and the sun missed her glow.

So, slowly the little sky angel
spread her wings to go.

As the woman wept and realized
that this could no longer be the
little sky angel's home.

Nestling in the clouds, the little sky angel settled back into her first home.

There, she watched the woman hold onto their melodies from before.

Author's Note

I wrote this book as a poem, a place to heal, an ode to the life and loss of a friend's Little Sky Angel, Akindejoye. The late daughter of one of my closest friends who inspired my life with her love, vulnerability, resilience, perseverance, and joy. She allowed me to share her testimony to honor the lives of all mothers, families, and children here and in heaven. It is with admiration, love, faith, and at times a heavy heart that may have brought us all here to this place of reading her story. Thank you for being an amazing friend and for allowing me to share in your place of healing.

With love,

Chenna

A Note from Akindejoye's Mom

"God has blessed me with my rainbow baby. I know my Little Sky Angel is watching over her little sister. I miss you, my sweet baby girl. I know I will see you again one day. Until then, keep enjoying heaven until mommy gets there."

I love you,

Ginger Ndidi Unegbu

www.ingramcontent.com/pod-product-compliance
Lightning Source LLC
Chambersburg PA
CBHW042055060526
44119CB00118B/322